Tacenda Literary Magazine

2017 Edition

Editor-In-Chief
Daniella Sklarz

Consulting Editor
Robert Johnson

Cover Design
Casey Chiappetta

Text Design
Sonia Tabriz

BleakHouse Publishing
2017

Ward Circle Building 254
American University
Washington, DC 20016

NEC Box 67
New England College
Henniker, New Hampshire 03242
www.BleakHousePublishing.com

Robert Johnson – Editor & Publisher
Sonia Tabriz - Managing Editor
Liz Calka - Creative Director

Casey Chiappetta – Chief Operating Officer
Daniella Sklarz – Chief Editorial Officer
Emily Dalgo – Chief Development Officer
Rachel Ternes – Chief Creative Officer

Jacob Bray – Art Director
Shirin Karimi – Senior Creative Consultant

Copyright © 2017 by Robert Johnson

All rights reserved. No part of this book shall be reproduced or transmitted in any form or by any means, electronic, mechanical, magnetic, photographic including photocopying, recording or by any information storage and retrieval system, without prior written permission of the publisher. No patent liability is assumed with respect to the use of the information contained herein. Although every precaution has been taken in the preparation of this book, the publisher and author assume no responsibility for errors or omissions. Neither is any liability assumed for damages resulting from the use of the information contained herein.

ISBN: 978-0-9961162-3-7

Printed in the United States of America

A Note From the Editor

TACENDA: n., pronounced ta'KEN'da
'things better left unsaid'

TACENDA: n., pronounced ta'KEN'da
'things better left unsaid'

Within our criminal justice system, one of the worst atrocities is the silencing of those who live behind bars. To be human is to have a voice; a voice that is free to shout, sing, laugh. It humanizes the speaker and challenges the reader to confront a system and cycle of deprivation of liberty and freedom.

But all too often, voices of prisoners and their advocates are silenced. At Tacenda, we believe in the power of words and the importance of being heard. We know that a person's voice can be heard from the page. The words of the authors in this collection speak volumes.

To move forward is to foster understanding and to embrace empathy for those whose lives can fall through the cracks of the criminal justice system. Through these works of poetry and fiction and prose, we hope to honor and promote human dignity and justice, to look passed labels like "criminal" or "convict" and instead see the humanity of those affected by our justice system.

We must document the experiences of those silenced by the justice system so that the present may inform a just future. We must listen. From this listening, we must speak up against injustice, informed by the stories of those most affected.

We believe this collection can give us all a chance to listen and learn from one another.

Table of Contents

Prison Phone Calls	Maureen Geraghty	8
Generations	Kari Lorentson	9
Empathizing with Darkness	Lawrence Green	10
Accumulation	Emily Dalgo	11
Slavishly We Follow	Josef Krebs	12
Cyclical	Lucas Chapman	13
Drunks: Relapse	Rick Lyon	14
Stand-Up Man	Gary Leaks	15
Hamster Wheel	Khalid Karim	16
10-12 Year-Olds	Dortell Williams	17
From Your Sister, Karen	Naomi Zeigler	18
Billions of Prisons	Jevon Jackson	20
Two Trees	Anonymous	21
Guilty	Sarah Bousquet	22
The Sin of Omission	Nick Leininger	23
Play Pretend	Daniella Sklarz	24
The Discarded Rag Doll	Anna Hassanyeh	26
Dreams	Emily Dalgo	31

Longing	Timothy Tingle-Brown	32
Pleasures	Lucas Chapman	33
Not Guilty	Sarah Bousquet	34
Suddenly	Josef Krebs	36
Employer	Kari Lorentson	37
I Will Cry For The Little Boy	Halim Flowers	38
America	Alazajuan Gray	39
If	Jean Marc Akerele	41
Freedom & Fantasy	Nastasya Popov	42
The Difference Between Dr. King and Me	Sincere Echoes	46
Containment	Hannah Ehlers	48
We, The Imprisoned Free	Maureen Geraghty	49
The Unthinkable Pt. 1	Ryan Newman	50
Drunks: Return	Rick Lyon	51
Here Again	Lydell Clanton	52
Caught	Nancy Tolley	53
Clichés	Sarah Bousquet	57
Fertile Concrete	Gary Leaks	58
Lost Souls	Kwame Bias	59

Bad Actors: Sad, Very Sad	Robert Johnson	60
Friend or Foe	Khalid Karim	66
The Lockdown	Jevon Jackson	68
A Collection of Sonnets from Death Row	Anthony G. Amsterdam	70

Prison Phone Calls
Maureen Geraghty

"To accept charges, press one..."
One. One. Pressing one to reach two.
We subsist on wireless connection,
speak spoonfuls of Freedom doled out
in fifteen minute servings.
We must love, fight, explain and inform
within irritating interruptions.
"This call may be recorded for security purposes..."

A call, a lifeline to a world un-made of metal & fluorescent light
Here, we learn to touch in tenderly crafted words,
translate subtext of tone & pause.
This is sacred space where voices wear no uniform,
numbers are not names.

"Your calls may be monitored..."
Punching, punching holes in fragile balloon of sanctuary,
ever threatening privacy
so we weave our curtain of confidential
sip each syllable, hold shared thoughts tightly
as children cling to coins, to a mother's hand.

"You have one minute left."
Fumbling to wrap up
what we've so tenderly unpacked.
Rushing where we want to linger
Only seconds left of God.

Generations
Kari Lorentson

I am.
Inmate 35-09888.
Spitting image of my mother.
Inmate 254-09473.
Grandma is my #1 fan.
Inmate 225-07433.

Not quite
the family reunion
I envisioned under the
gazebo at the park
with the stable shade of
mature oaks.

More like a get-together
interrupted by intruding cameras and
blinding sun flare from barbed-wired.

I have
Three children.
Born as infant inmates
Just like their mother.

I'm the branch
Of a rotten family tree
But what chance did I have?
The roots are sour
My kids.
Product of poisonous pollination.
They'll never sprout.

Empathizing with Darkness
Lawrence Green

Someone once shared with me
The darkness behind these walls
Like being surrounded by piranhas
And bone crushing shark jaws

Every time he re-entered society
A new story was told with a smile
It was hard to receive a lesson
When expressions seem to guide

No one wants to die in prison
And certainly doesn't want to waste their fine
No one wants to come out an old man
After entering darkness in their prime

The day that darkness surrounded me
Understanding became so clear
It's hard to control your emotions
When your freedom is near and dear

I finally share his feelings
Cause I know from which he speak
I appreciate his strength
Cause it didn't make him weak

Accumulation
Emily Dalgo

When it disguises itself as late nights,
Procrastination,
Cancelled plans,
It's easy to forget and forgive.

When it dresses itself in pajamas, cozy socks,
Soft blankets,
It's easy to welcome it inside.

When it tries to get you to play,
Pens, open windows, and forks from your unwashed pasta bowl
Start to look like toys.

When it creeps back into your soul,
Silently and slowly,
Isolation, pity, and panic

Look a lot less comfortable
Than peace.
Than death.

Slavishly We Follow Our Predicament
Josef Krebs

Slavishly we follow our predicament
As if it were only circumstance
Instead of a path we had chosen

Cyclical
Lucas Chapman

Round and round the black eyes go,
and where they'll stop nobody knows
First punch I got was six years old
for reaching in the cookie bowl

Age nine, got hit cause I caught blame
for jinxing daddy's football game.
At twelve, teachers questioning the bruise-
Told them I fell, invent a ruse
so they wouldn't know
I had only tried to hide mom's booze.

Well mom's on meth and dad is too
so I guess they never could have knew
their little girl at age thirteen
would quickly turn so cold and mean

I was only copying what they showed me
and I wish somebody would have told me
fists are no tools for communication
who knew that'd lead to my incarceration.

Yeah, the girls in prison show me love
but I only know how to push and shove
with shaved head, tattoos and emotions set aside
I keep hidden inside the girl who died.

Round and round the black eyes go,
but they ended my life a long time ago.

Drunks: Relapse
Rick Lyon

Moth to the flame, she can't leave the stuff alone,
stole the tequila from under our noses,
not that we cared, the little left in the bottle,
but why would you risk the job, the children,
recently reunited after her previous overdose;
or is it only another stop on the cycle of sickness,
repeating itself, varying its contours,
as if it's different this time, when everyone knows it isn't.
And when will it be enough, punishing oneself, -
killing oneself?
It makes no sense, which is the sense it makes,
perfect sense, no sense,
the crying and moaning and helplessness.
No surprise she winds up at the hospital.
Booze and blood pressure medication
bring her to her knees, a final reckoning.
One's comforted, almost, in knowing
the moth will always circle the flame, always,
until daylight drowns out the light, -
drowns out the darkness,
which is all one hoped for anyway,
some surfeit, some fullness and plentitude
in an empty world, perfect sense.

Stand-Up Man
Gary Leaks

When the cuffs get clamped on
We don't perform . . .
We don't point fingers
We don't become R&B singers . . .
We embrace whatever adversity bring us
Brought me - Taught me -
To stand firm on my pivotal
During conditions, which is critical
During situations, which is political
I pled the 5th . . . Amendment right as a gift
Knowing that the 13th was my burden
Of that, I was 99.2% certain
Flirting . . . with death as I take each step
Because the path towards freedom
has always been stalked by the reaper
word play potent as the strongest reefer
and I can refer you to some potent literature
But the question is . . . will you read it?
My answer is "hell yeah"
If you ask me, do you need it ?
Vanity is the identical twin of conceited
For whom, who know it all
Will you ever grow at all?
Stand up man standing tall
. . .I AM . . .

Hamster Wheel
Khalid Karim

Chow Call! Chow Call!
To the mess hall we go for sustenance
School Call! School Call!
To get an education that could be of sustenance
Rec Call! Rec Call!
Everyone heads to the yard in abundance.
Count Time! Count Time!
We move slowly, to our cells with reluctance.
Chow call!
School call!
Rec call!
Count time!
Chow call!
School call!
Rec call!
Count time!
and now we go to sleep
in hopes of being freed in a dream
a dream that's more precious than reality.
Chow time!
School Time!
Rec Call!
Count Time!
And on and on and on
this is the hamster wheel of mine
and of many, many more
the hamster wheel of time.

10 – 12 Year-Olds
Dortell Williams

How is it, my dear
a misguided youth of 10-to-12 years
can be corrupted by adults or his peers?
In that short span of say, 2 years;
an urban generational fate
from the playground to the police
and then prison the gate.
Tossed away with an eternal date;
warehoused for perpetual profit
in the bloodied hands of the state.
The irony is clear, no doubt
a dearth of rehabilitation, a lack of reform.
Nothing whatsoever to tour.
Redemption in the military, rehab centers and churches churn
Yet CDCR fails dismally to teach or even learn.
30 years-plus it takes to reform 2 years of corruption.
It's a farce, it's an outrage
Claiming to rehabilitate humans in a cage.
There's another model that far exceeds abroad,
Google Germany, Switzerland
Or Norway's prisons and grant the not
You want public safety, human and morality wrapped in one and tame?
Stop the insanity, the profanity and inhumane shame!

From Your Sister, Karen
Naomi Zeigler

You used to make me laugh at my birthday parties
your antics letting me forget
how it felt when Dad would hit me
liquor on his breath and fire in his eyes
the birthday cake you made for me crashing to the floor

I cried when Mom found out you stole the toy truck
for me from the neighborhood store
and the whimpers you tried so hard to conceal
when Dad beat you with his belt
and told you that you would never be good enough

Sometimes when I hear them say your name on the news
all I can remember is your garden
you planted every flower so tenderly as if the soil
was the most sacred and holy ground
because it meant that something could grow

And you tried so hard to grow like the garden you planted
but all you were given was the blistering sun
the words Dad said under his breath
then escaping out loud after one or two drinks
and the way he hit you till you could not longer see

I wish I would not have found out your love for men
from the pages of the newspapers
or the way our family friend would touch you
and keep you in his grasp and would not let you go
even though you tried to scream and cry

They found the men you loved underneath your- floorboards
was it your way to hold on to twenty six men
who you could love in secret and silence
could it be that you were so ashamed
my brother, who were you to them?

You shook Rosalynn Carter's hand in the burgundy suit
that you bought with the money you made
and the friends that you had who believed you were good
And you made them laugh like you made me laugh
your face painted in a smile, trying to recreate your youth

I wanted to believe you were innocent for so long
and all I would remember was the way you tucked me in
late at night to keep my nightmares at bay
how was it that you could save me from my fears
but become a monster yourself when the sun went down

Oh my brother, John, your name means
"God is gracious," but He was not gracious to you
Will your children ever reply to the letters I send to them
every year on the anniversary of your death
they send them back to me unopened, unread

I imagine one day you come back to me
and I cannot seem to piece together the parts
of the car that you helped me buy when we were young
and your gentle hands fix the mess and I know you love me
and you would know that I forgive you

John Wayne Gacy, Jr. was born in Illinois. Convicted of murdering thirty three young men, he was executed by lethal injection on May 10, 1994. He was survived by his mother, two sisters, and two children.

Billions of Prisons
Jevon Jackson

We're all doing time,
somewhere out in an open field
there are hell hounds chasing us
down
deep into the bottom dirt,

whether we're covered in addictions
or greed, malfeasance
or abuse, vanity
or infidelity, hatred
or untruths

we run like a muthafucker

no matter what sin we're in
we just wanna run
till' we survive
so we can make it
home
in one piece.

Two Trees
Anonymous

Outside my cell window, I can see two trees
Green, spry, and borne by the love of an emerald green field.
To the one, the other made his branches rustle
As they do in a thunderstorm of a thousand different colors.
To the other, the one made her leaves shudder
From nervousness, fear, or excitement—
Who can tell?
Yet watching these two arboreal friends with their branchy fingers reaching high,
Growing together and learning the limits of the sky,
I'm sadly struck by the lead imitation trees barring me from outside.

Guilty
Sarah Bousquet

It was the screaming.
They always ask
What made me do it
My lawyer says
Stay silent, hold remorse
But it was the screaming.

No matter how many times
I said,
"Stop crying, baby;
Mommy's here'

It wouldn't stop screaming

And I could feel it in my soul
Reverberating around my skull
I couldn't even hear myself think

She was in pain
She wanted me to
It wouldn't shut up

And I was going crazy
I think I still am
Because even after she's gone
And I had my silence,
The screaming I felt inside
Didn't stop.

The Sin of Omission
Nick Leininger

Not choosing is a choice
Prisoners aren't given a voice
Laborers void of a vote and void of a hope

Laying stonework for the powerful's pyramids
Serfs digging their own graves
Watched over by the pontiffs of the almighty dollar

How can we trust those who watch them?
Who will police the police?
Who will watch the watchmen?

If it's really only a few bad apples
Why do they all seem to fall from the same tree?
Even Eden must be held accountable for her strange fruit

Today, people are held in bondage for plant possession
Executed for suspicious behavior
Enslaved on the basis of their shade
Castaways, cast away from the light of day
Forced to reside in the dark

I mourn for the meek but not for the weak
The meek shall inherit the earth
The weak shall inherit the dirt

When good has no champion, evil reigns supreme

Play Pretend
Daniella Sklarz

If this was play pretend
I would be seven and you would be five
I would be wearing a uniform with a badge
And you would have on black and white stripes

If this was play pretend
I would be very mean and tell you, "YOU ARE BAD"
I would say you are here to be a better person
But can you be a better person?

If this was play pretend
I would give you a plate of mush and say to close your eyes
So that you didn't know where it came from
And make you eat it, even with the smell

If this was play pretend
I would not let you see mom and dad
Or brother
Or Patches

If this was play pretend
I would lock you in the closet and turn off the lights
Shut down the heat to make it cold
And not open when you knock and beg

If this was play pretend
I would take away all your toys
Because you cannot be entertained
Because you should be bored

But if this was play pretend
After a little bit of play

I would give you

A pretty dress
A big hug
Some cookies
A blanket
My favorite toy
And we'd all laugh

But these walls have no room
For pondering possibilities
This isn't play
And certainly, not pretend.

The Discarded Ragdoll
Anna Hassanyeh

That morning, Buck, one of Momma's boyfriends, sauntered into the kitchen shirtless and wearing scruffy jeans. He clicked his tongue and shook his head when he saw me sipping from a bottle of liquor left from the night before.

'You is too young to be drinking,' he said, placing an unlit cigarette between his dry lips. His front teeth were missing, the short hair on his face crept down his neck towards a thin dusting of chest hair. His mottled skin stretched across his ribs and his stomach concaved like a stray dog's.

'Have you paid?' I asked, ignoring his last comment. Momma's boyfriends pay her when they visit, but sometimes they forget. The tiny-scabbed holes in his arm stretched as he reached into his back pocket pulling out a wad of dog-eared dollar bills. My hand instinctively rested on the handle of the kitchen drawer, the one that contained Momma's handgun.

'I'll give you forty bucks,' he said. The cigarette hung limply from his lips and flapped as the words left his mouth.

'Make it fifty,' I said.

His eyes narrowed. 'Fine,' he said.

I snatched the money and took ten dollars for myself, not for clothes or magazines, but for food, something nice, not the usual TV dinners.

'How old are you?' Buck asked, taking a flimsy matchbook from his pocket. He flipped the book open and pulled out a matchstick. The matchstick scratched against the striker and the flame fizzled to life, dancing amber upon the tip then fading to blue against the wood.

'Fifteen.'

Buck flicked the match onto the floor and removed the cigarette from his lips; smoke tumbled from his nose and mouth and his eyes travelled up my legs. I tightened my grip on the drawer handle.

'Tell your momma I'll be back Friday.'

I nodded and he walked out of the kitchen. The rickety front door opened then rattled shut.

'Caitlin?'

Like a contortionist, my stomach twisted at the sound of Momma's rasping voice. She was leaning against the doorframe, an empty bottle of vodka in one hand and a cigarette in the other. Her cheeks were hollow and smudged eyeliner made her eyes two black tunnels leading to a speck of blue sky. Her blonde hair, which had once been healthy and strong, was now a limp and greasy curtain across her face. Her skin was a patchwork of caked foundation, too dark for her pale skin.

'Get Momma a drink.'

'You've had enough.'

'Don't get sassy with me,' she seethed.

Momma was not always such a hateful creature; however, after Poppa left, Momma stopped doing much of anything, except for smoking and drinking and blaming.

'When's Tomas coming over?' I asked. Tomas is another of Momma's boyfriends. I liked Tomas. When I was eight years old he bought me an old ragdoll, which I loved. I'd hold onto that ragdoll and Tomas would bounce me up and down on his lap and tickle me all over. We would laugh until our stomachs hurt, but things change, people change. Eventually, Momma threw away the ragdoll. She said I'd become too attached, that it wasn't a good thing to love something so much.

'Tomas is coming later,' Momma grumbled as I passed her the dollar bills.

'You giving *all* the money to him?'

There was a flicker of sadness in her face, and then her eyes hardened.

'Isn't it about time you started paying your own way?' She licked her lips. 'I'm sure Tomas can sort something out; his clients have been asking about you, anyways.'

The thought of taking after Momma felt as if ice-cold water had been poured into my veins. I knew she didn't care much, but I never thought she would deliver me fresh to the slaughterhouse.

Later that day, I made my way to Randy's house. Despite being ten years older than me, Randy had always treated me special. After a glass of coke, Randy set up three empty cans on an old tree stump in his backyard. I was never keen on shooting, but Randy liked guns and wanted to teach me. I couldn't say no. Randy passed me his air pellet rifle and I shot down the first can but missed the second. He stood behind me and placed his hands on my waist, bringing his mouth close to my ear. I wanted to turn my head and place my lips against his, but bravery was a trait that often eluded me.

'Think about someone that wronged you,' he said. I aimed the rifle and thought of Momma. 'Give'em what they deserve and shoot'em good.'

Randy stepped back and I pulled the trigger. The pellet pierced a tidy hole through the second can. He whooped, placing a proud arm around my shoulders. I nuzzled my face into the crook of his neck, breathing in his familiar scent.

'Randy!' A woman's voice called. I jumped from Randy's embrace and saw a tall, blonde woman walking towards us wearing a flowing red dress, which was bunched tightly at the waist. Her shiny red heels made it hard for her to walk across the pitted soil, so she held out her pale, slender arms to keep her balance. I glanced at Randy whose smile was so big that the corners of his eyes crinkled.

'Lucy,' Randy said, walking towards her. He held the woman in a tight embrace and kissed her intensely on the lips. I was pathetic in my faded jeans and t-shirt. Everything about Lucy was better than me. Her hair was blonder, her eyes bluer. I clutched onto the rifle.

'Come and meet, Caitlin,' Randy said.

'Hi, Caitlin.' Lucy smiled. I shook the hand she offered me. 'Randy's told me so much about you. You're such a sweet girl.' My jaw tightened at the word *girl*. That's what the problem was, I was a girl and she was a woman.

Randy filled the dreadful silence: 'Caitlin's great with a gun. Shoot the last can.' He gestured towards me. I aimed the rifle at the lonesome can; I shot straight through its heart, splitting it in two.

It was late afternoon when I went home to check on Momma. Tomas was sitting on one of the kitchen chairs, his ankles crossed and resting on the table. His brown-leather cowboy hat was dipped low, creating a mysterious shadow across his eyes. He held a few green notes in his hand. The ten dollars I stole weighed heavy in my pocket.

'I've got forty dollars.' His voice was smooth and deep with a hint of incrimination.

'Buck said he paid fifty.'

'Maybe he counted his money wrong.' I shrugged.

Tomas swept his feet off the table and stood. He was a towering giant, but I held his gaze. I didn't realize what was happening until I was on the floor with Tomas' shined-up shoes kicking into my stomach over and over. He pulled me up by my wrist and I couldn't breathe. He dug into my pockets until he found the ten-dollar bill. He held it to my face. The air from my gasping lungs fluttered the green paper like a leaf in the wind.

'You know, Caitlin, your Momma said you're ready to start earning your own money.' Tomas' breath smelled of stale beer and old smoke and I began wailing like a wounded wolf when he pulled at my jeans. I tried to stop him. I tried to edge my way to the kitchen drawer that contained the handgun, but his strong hands held, unyielding, against my body. I grabbed onto an empty white cup, which rested on the kitchen counter. I attempted to smash it across his head, but the cup slipped from my sweaty fingertips and shattered into a million pieces on the floor. I used to think Tomas was one of the kind ones, but what he did to me, on that kitchen floor, was far from it. I whipped my arms and legs and pleaded for Momma until my throat burned raw. When I realized she wasn't coming, I pleaded for anything else but this, that I was sorry, that I didn't want to be a prostitute like Momma.

Eventually, I stopped fighting. Instead, I thought of Randy and how he'd never want me now. I closed my eyes and listened to my erratic breathing, hopelessly eradicating the chorus of ghastly noises and horrid names that bounced off the walls and seeped into my soul.

When Tomas had finished, I lay motionless on the kitchen floor. He tossed me the ten dollars and said that to deserve money, I needed to earn it. That's when Momma came.

'Momma.' I reached out a trembling hand. I needed her to pick up the pieces, to kiss me better, the way mommas are supposed to. My empty hand dropped to the floor.

'He raped me,' I said. My voice was raspy and filled with disbelief. I hoped the words would jolt Momma into action. I imagined her screaming at Tomas to leave, then cradling me in her arms, but her eyes stared blankly at the smudges of blood on my thighs. I'll never forget the look in her eyes. Bare. Hollow. Like a discarded ragdoll. Like skilled puppeteers, rage and betrayal coaxed me to my feet and guided my hand to the kitchen drawer.

That night, Detective Tucker sits behind his desk at the Windshaw County Police Station. Beads of perspiration cling to his top lip and sweat teases the thin grey hairs at the back of his neck. There is a complicated smell of pine, stale sweat and something distinctly spicy; the concoction is strong enough to make my eyes water. Tucker has two framed pictures hanging in his office, one with the American flag and another of him with a bald eagle perched on his gloved hand. The eagle's accusing eyes glare at me from the photograph, its beak gripping a cut of dead meat.

Tucker sighs and his right hand traces a pen across a page in his notebook, containing details of my every move since the beginning of the interview. I glimpse a few, indiscriminate words: *young, tearful, pale, underweight.* He sits back in his chair.

'Caitlin, a statement could help your case.'

I nod.

Tucker's smile is kind. He reaches for a wireless cassette recorder and places it on the table. There are five buttons: record, play, pause, forward and rewind. I stare at the rewind button, wishing I could rewind my entire life and start again. Tucker presses record and a red light flashes four times before remaining steady.

After stating my name, the date and the time, Tucker turns to me: 'Caitlin, please detail the events at your home on Saturday May 8th.' He waits. The only sounds are the tape uncoiling and recoiling, a faint static, and Tucker's intermittent breathes. I sigh and begin the account of the day I murdered my mother.

Dreams
Emily Dalgo

I felt the warmth of your chest

On my bare back

I felt the beat of your heart

One two

Three

I felt the curve of your legs

Tucked between mine

Tangled

Lost

Coloring book bodies

Lines blurred

I can't tell

Where you end and I begin

Longing
Timothy Tingle-Brown

She looks into his eyes
And he can see that she
Has fallen into the depths
Of them,
Likewise,
He has fallen into the
Same Chocolate pools that
Which are theirs,
They share.
Home her hero has finally
Come,
In his arms his princess
Is finally embraced,
No longer long lost loves,
Then he awakens,
Lonely,
And Saddened, in search
Of that lovely but heart breaking
Dream, in which he could
See his daughter again....

Pleasures
Lucas Chapman

Showers
once meant solitude
cleanliness, warmth
preparation for a night out
And now they are dozens of eyes watching me
comments on my breasts
cold, filthy, maxi pads on my feet and hair in the drain
Food
once was freedom of flavor
fourth of July burgers and mom's lasagna
dinner dates and cookouts
whole pigs and fresh fruit
And now?
cans marked "Desert Storm"
always leaving hungry
a struggle of mold and meat
having only Ramen noodles to cling to as a reminder that I did, at some point, enjoy this.
Sex
was a comfort of love
but now it's hurried, cold and passionless
an expression of dominance, an assertion of her over I
a transaction, like at commissary
The little pleasures that once were little pleasures are pleasures no more.

Not Guilty
Sarah Bousquet

She wasn't always a ghost
But time had eroded her
Chipped away little pieces of her soul
She could feel her voice fading
Her mind,
fading

And her desire to be touched
Long gone
She used to wish
For just a hand to hold hers
But there is nothing left of her
To hold

And she stands,
When they tell her,
Sits where they tell her
But they don't bother telling her
Anymore

Her lawyer stopped his calls
As he stopped believing her innocence
And soon his name was a distant memory
And she faded
A little more

She gave up wishing
On shooting stars
And she gave up wanting
And as she finally
Gave up hope

She became
Just another ghost
Dead eyes and dead heart
Another number,

Nothing more.

Suddenly
Josef Krebs

Suddenly
Nothing is sudden
All the spring is lost
Faces don't match up to named
Irresponsibility is no longer fun
Pieces don't fit into pieces
And the center was always lost
Created by ambition to be someone
Until all is illuminated by crisis of conscience
Particular to who is particular
'Til we all run down
And nothing is left
But dust and resonance

Employer
Kari Lorentson

We're hiring!
Entry level positions with solid pay are available now.
Open interview will be held all-day Monday.

They asked me questions about experience.
I told them about my food service days,
just not where I learned my skills.
They asked me about my reliability.
I told them I've never been late to shifts,
just not that the daily 5am would would wake me up.
They asked me why I was applying.
I told them I just relocated and am looking for a job,
Just not that I used to be a number, not a name.

We'd like to have you join the team
      they told me.
Please fill out this form and we'll call you tomorrow.

Race/Ethnicity?
      African American
Veteran Status? Check Yes or No
      Yes
Convicted of a Felony? Check Yes or No
      Yes

The manager called this morning.
Rejected.

I Will Cry for the Little Boy
Halim Flowers

I will cry for the little boy
In shackles and away from home
I will cry for the little boy
Trapped in a cell all alone

I will cry for the little boy
Whose heart is too cold to weep
I will cry for the little boy
Pain never lets him sleep

I will cry for the little boy
He was buried alive in the burning sand
I will cry for the little boy
The boy sentenced to life like a man

I will cry for the little boy
Who knows his soul is in chains
I will cry for the little boy
His spirit died again and again

I will cry for the little boy
A good boy he tried to be
I will cry for the little boy
That died inside of me

America, it's safe to say, all your blood, sweat, and tears has paved the way, so the next generation, can have it better than we have it today. I close my eyes, and take some time to realize, what matters is all lives.

America
By Alazajuan Gray

The story of freedom always was a work of art
A picture perfect dream that melted my heart,
We defeated the odds
We as a nation seen our first black president
In the land of the free, and I'm proud to be a resident
Everlasting victory, we made classic history
But as of Nov. 2016 we are now back in misery
Man, I ask God to turn this demonic night back to day
open our eyes and see things His way
We all are blinded by our own desires
And the hate is spreading burning like wildfires
Is this the ugly future we want our kids to face
Grow up and be mistreated, because of their race
This is a disgrace, we all should be ashamed
Democrats, and Republicans we all are the blame
This campaign was the spark to the flame
I hope this poem becomes the reader novocaine
It's time to wake up before it's too late to make up
Hate to see my country so divided, one track minded
selfish, secluded, and confine.
Without compassion, and empathy as our sight
We will remain channeled, static and black and white
America the great, a beautiful democracy
has flip to hate and hypocrisy
One Election set off the detection
of constant oppression, race neglection
Religion rejection, to separation
immigration, kids scared of deportation
Damn, we all need reflection, a lil' god meditation

Because prayer is the only medication
to the hurtful situation

God bless America

If
Jean Marc Akerele

If prisons
Lease our liberty

If seas
Rent our shores

If silence
Hustles penny songs

If power
Purchases helplessness

Then into this world
I step renewed

To float unbound
Cocooned in pleasure, in pain

Not yet spent
Comprehend, contained

A desperate paradigm
Unknown, unborn, untainted

If this time
I can love myself enough to live

Freedom & Fantasy
Nastasya Popov

For the first time in five years, Alla's husband was confronted with his own freedom. Assuredness he had none. The outside world was to him a selfie-obsessed hive of evil, vibrant with a malignant narcissism that he could not understand, or the comfortable place of beauty that his family inhabited, which he did not anymore deserve. After the initial elation of physically owning his body and stepping out into the Long Beach, sulfur infused air, the pair quickly learned that true freedom is a but a concept, a fantasy.

At the time of his incarceration five years before, he had just recently stopped drinking, heavily, for the first time since teenage hood; had found spirituality in prison, and now meditated every day and taught a spiritual healing class to other inmates. The gray circles under his eyes were pronounced in the morning light. He wore a gray sweat suit. Alla's pixie cut stuck out as too contemporary for the surroundings. She never wore makeup, her face clean as the minimalistic designs she thought up. *She presented a naked white countenance to the faultfinding light of* July. Her husband, upon returning home, would for the first time read his dead mother Valentina's journals, which Alla had rescued for him from Moscow after Valentina's death, and find out that his mother had abandoned him before he turned one.

That Monday morning, July 25th, his release date, everything opposed Alla's expectations. The Correctional Officer who let her in was mean (this part was expected), not allowing her to wait in the lot adjacent to the prison, so she parked in the Fire Station's lot nearby. Her rearview mirror was small, so when her husband did walk out, she saw a mini figure and had to guess as to whether it was time for her to run towards him in ecstasy. She knew it was right when the mean officer's voice yelled, "Popov, over there!" While running, she screamed "Sasha" and he stood there, face frozen, stiff, without saying a word.

---

[1] Vladimir Nabokov, Symbols and Signs.

At the car, she watched him jump inside, on edge, eager for her to start driving. One of the other visitors glanced into the car as she walked by, recognized them, recognized his release, and shouting "Congrats!" Sasha curled inward at the exclamation. He asked whether Alla had brought the Andrey Makarevich CD he had requested. She had. She burned it off of her computer because it was not online. He looked at his gray CD case lovingly, putting the CD in, letting the music overcome the silence, and stared straight forward as Alla drove.

During the long ride home in LA's traffic, she and her husband hardly exchanged a word. She was surprised, but accepting. She wasn't going to push him. In this sense, the ride and the first few months were very hard for her. Less difficult, possibly, than the period during which he had
attempted to drink himself to death with a masterpiece of dramatic episodes that included living in an apartment that used to be Charlie Chaplin's, which he plainly could not afford, or getting engaged to a woman who looked nothing like Angelina Jolie, even though she tried her best.

Later that week, he wanted them to go to the water. To eat in Malibu, put their feet in the sand, enjoy their seafood, feel the ocean, drive home, arrive at the halfway
house on time, and somehow avoid the pulsing tension in the air. Their reality was a series of sporadic movements and a nonexistent fluidness between point A and point B.

When he arrived home, he breathed for a moment. He loved what she had done with the apartment. He put his netted, prison satchel anywhere, which bothered Alla. She was particular about how things were set up in her household. She was very independent and had her own way of curating her space. The bag reeked of the place and he put it on the wooden, butterflied dining room table. Her aversion to the bag was palpable, but she would quietly move it to the corner by the door. In the company of her well-worn solitaire deck that night, she decided she would go to Good Will and buy him a replacement bag the next day, so that he couldn't protest about her spending too much on clothing for him.

He rejected anything that he was not familiar with. Cell phones, Facebook, Quiet. "How much was it?" he would ask about the replacement bag, "only a few dollars," she would insist. She wanted him to forget about it, to pretend like it had never happened, but he would talk about prison often and this upset her. Her daughter would soon remind her that her father had only known a singular building for five years. That this building was his world for that long. What else did he have to reminisce on?

He had come out expecting the pace of life to be slow. To sit down with people, to discuss things. He didn't understand the rhythm of the world he reentered. Everyone was in a rush, incommunicative. He learned to leave people alone, to give up his fantasies of spending time with his friends and family, ruminating on life like Greek or Roman philosophers.

To Alla, it almost sounded like he would prefer to be back in prison. Back to his routine of meditating in the morning and then biking for an hour on a stationary cycle. Back to law and order. He was often complaining about lack of exercise, about being cooped up, "stagnant" as he called it. Other wives told her of their experiences during this phase where grown men act like frightened children. Stella's husband, Michael, had driven their minivan without stopping for hours until they were far enough from the prison for him to breathe. Sasha's past bunkie, a tattooed, ex-Marine named Emanuel, had wept as they crossed the bridge leaving Terminal Island, where the prison was located.

"Are you going to ask me what I like about coming back?" my dad asks me six months after those initial, foreign memories of release.

"Sure, tell me." I say.

"I like everything. Life here is full of beauty and without restriction. The world is full of beautiful people and beautiful nature and beautiful places and beautiful things."

"I didn't ask you that because I already knew you felt that way. I've felt you feel that way." And so had my mother, Alla.

"Okay, good." Beat. "Oh, and one more thing that I want to add—my relationship and feelings towards my family became my first priority [upon release.] I now feel a responsibility towards my family's well-being and peace above all else."

"Okay, Papa, thank you. I understand."
"Good. Now get back to your homework."

The Difference Between Dr. King and Me
Sincere Echoes

I don't believe this is the dream Dr. King had for me
Somewhere along the timeline, my decisions rewrote history
My choices had voices
Those senseless noises shoulda been avoided

But here's the difference...
When King was taking a stand and marchin' for a cause
I was taking a fall and wasn't marchin' at all
Couldn't cover the distance of 3 days and 54 miles, in search of a vision
That the march on Selma, for those who didn't get it

King stood for peace
While I stood for the streets, which lead me to a place I no longer wanna be
His life brought us Civil Rights
And I sold my freedom to time
Those decades are now deceased and laid to rest in my mind

King will forever be a legend
While my reputation seems life it's not worth remembering
When my baby momma showed a picture to my child and asked
"Do you remember him?"
I was a strange face to them

King sold a belief that lifted more lives than I put down on concrete
He moved a nation
I moved to any cell that was vacant
King was an activist, a philanthropist
I was on the active list of warrants that only a felon can get

We both had mug shot faces with a rap sheet
King's rap sheet bled through with integrity
When he was assassinated on a balcony
My rap sheet, bleeds ink, when you read about the worst in me
That a character suicide cause I made up my mind

That I was gonna do or die and that frame of mind
Will never lead me to a Nobel Peace Prize

King's leadership paved a way with the potential to be great
My leadership dug graves, where I laid my potential to waste
He prayed for better days
I prayed for a better way when it all seemed grey

While King was trying to reconstruct a nation and bring an end to segregation
I'm in the pen politickin', ready to ride on other races and bring an end to segregation
Situation into a permanent placement
He tried to educate us
I wasn't trying to be educated enough

King was dream chasin' and I was chasin' a buck
That's penniless sense that no longer adds up

Now here's the big difference between King and me
I'm living this nightmare and King died for the dream

I think it's time to wake up and make the change and redirect the course of things

Containment
Hannah Ehlers

this is not reform

and if this is retribution
it's the wrong kind

this is guaranteed recidivism
and institutionalized
racism

these are non-violent offenders
these are mothers
separated from children
women never given a chance

these are mandatory minimums
for maximum pain

this is not working
this is a waste

of potential
of people
of life

this is a scream
echoing from cell to cell
a warning
bouncing off the bars:

be careful what you contain

We, the Imprisoned Free
Maureen Geraghty

We, the Imprisoned Free:
mothers,
lovers, children
and others.

We, the Imprisoned Free:
Co-confined within
barbed bureaucracy

We, the Imprisoned Free:
survive on collect calls,
short visits and long hauls
connect through buzzers & metal,
love across a plastic table.

We, the Imprisoned Free:
masters of loss, of waiting
do what we can, do without,
chew on worry,
starve on doubt.

We, the Imprisoned Free:
fifty thousand nights alone,
countless years on our own
the invisible loved ones,
shadows far away,
all the kids asking
and we don't know what to say.

We, the Imprisoned Free:
No Liberty,
Just us,
For We all.

The Unthinkable Pt. 1
Ryan Newman

Trapped in a place away from where I want to be
With feelings I dreaded, resurrected back and haunting me
Pandora's Box unlocked sat right in front of me
An empty space to fill it with whatever that I want it to be
How crazy it is it's you and me I'll rather see
Other than who's close to your heart that who's been wanting me
I feel guilty for these thoughts but the heart is the chooser
I feel wrong like when the help is becoming the user
The thoughts hurt in my head and it could be a tumor
The whispers you're hearing out love is in fact not a rumor
It's just some measures doesn't always equate to the ruler
Damn, how far will I sink before I start to choke?
How many burdens must be removed for me to come afloat?
How will I even get you to see beyond the scope?
How bout we both just go for what's certain and give up the hope?
Yeah, I think I like what is more than what isn't
And that's the feeling of your presence through these halls in prison
Without an option can you even make the best decision?
Without a problem will you even hear someone's opinion?
Huh! I guess rhetorical it is the most
Guess it's the memories I hear of you and not a ghost
I guess it's all safe to say than keep it bottled closed
A tattoo of your name
I did the unthinkable

Drunks: Return
Rick Lyon

Back from the cells, full of life,
bright clothes, bright hair, the perennial smile,
but dead in every way that matters,
spiritually, morally, emotionally spent,
soon to be a cypher, pure nothingness,
an empty space where a life once was.
She's already a ghost-like presence, unconvincing,
trying to convince, failing, and failing again.
One wishes to turn one's head away but can't,
waiting for the inevitable demolishment, annihilation,
which comes as no surprise to anyone
but the afflicted, oblivious,
and soon to be self-eradicated self.

Here Again
Lydell Clanton

I think I've been here before
Belly chains and ankle shackles
Stacked on top of each other
I just ate where I defecate
Is this 2016?
Or a New World southern state?
I think I've been here before
Hundreds of miles from my birthplace
Ain't seen a loved one in 10 years
Long days and a lot of tears
Death as a slave is my worst fear
I think I've been here before
Voices of abolitionist
Stories of freedom to the North
Stories of freedom through the courts!
Injustices rectified
Involuntary servitude nullifies
I think I've been here before
Arms linked in a show of unity
White and black alike
For justice, we march
For freedom, we fight
I think I've been here before
And we weathered the storm
I know I've been here before
And through strife is where
       victory will come

Caught
Nancy Tolley

The Plea
It wasn't just me- by my family you seem
      They're the ones who pushed me – to take the plea
The facts were there – but never presented,
      That's what deep down – I really resented.
I had no history – I'm the victim – yes, me,
      They only wanted – to push to a plea
A conviction is all – prosecutors go for,
      The truth really just- gets swept out the door.
It's over- I'm here – and to this day
      I never got it – I wish – I'd just had my say

Prison
They tell me to squat – spread um and cough,
      The system picked up – where my husband left off.
Five years is all – it could have been more,
      Some have gotten life – or years galore.
They say I'm blessed – but I can't see,
      I still wish – I had taken no plea.
Parole eligibility – in two and a half,
      It isn't funny – but I still got' a laugh.
Even if they give me – a little bit more,
      I cannot really see – what I'm in here for.

Degradation
Correctional institution's - degrade human life,
      Any positive existence – just isn't their strife.
Strip searching they start – when you walk in the door
      It's so frequent – just what are you doing this for.

At midnight – when you're in bed- asleep
      Is there something in there – we just need to peep,

Midnight urinalysis – they also do here,
      But their procedure – really seems kind of queer.
You strip – then they say – squat and cough,

They do this so much - they must really get off.
What about when - they make you pee
    Anything in there'd fall out - it would seem to me.

During a visit - I don't see how we're able,
    While sitting in a chair - our hands on the table.
To put anything inside our body - but don't you know,
    They search us again - from head to go.
Not only squat and cough - but run hands through your hair,
    For the privilege of a visit - got' a make sure -
    nothing's there.

Out of all the searches - how much do they find?
    Are drug use percentages - falling behind?
No - not really - usage is still on the rise,
    Shouldn't you reevaluate what you're doing there
    guys?
But no - part of the plan - is degradation,
    It's all part of - inmate demoralization.

Punishment
They say we are here to be punished - we need to repent,
    What they're really accomplishing - is to breed
    deep resent. .
For the system, that gives sentence - with no regard,
    To keep faith after this - itll really be hard.
Almost all in corrections - act better than thou,
    If this happened to them - they'd say thrown in the
    towel.
They say - change your life - get back on track,
    If you don't like it in here - then don't come back.

Things happen in life - its not always fair,
    If it doesn't affect them - they put you here,
Unless it happens to them - that thought won't veer.

No Peace in the Cell
I lay here and wait - time goes by,
    Read - write - find peace - or at least I try.
What am I waiting for - oh, I don't know,

Just hoping the guards will leave – just go.
Seems they bang the door – every half hour,
    Where do you think I am – like I really
    scour.
I'm locked in my cell – yet they constantly go by,
    Make noise at the door – have to see with their eye
We have to acknowledge them – in some kind of way,
    Or they'll just keep on – they won't go away.
If you are sleeping – don't move – or they think you ignore,
    They'll pull out their key – and open the door.

No Peace on the Grounds
I hate to go out – yet sometimes I must,
    The guards – their scrutiny – I just feel disgust.
Where's your ID – take that off – or – your out of bounds,
    The guards pick so much – some are nothing but
    hound
Across necklace – choke hazard – so flimsy they can see,
    Take it off – or ill take it – guards won't let it be.
Drop mail in the morning – on the way to school,
    Depends who you are – out bounds – you broke a
    rule.
Discrimination – bias – see it every day
    Stay low – don't say hi – keep outta their way.

No Peace When You Eat
When they call feed up – I try to be so fast,
    God forbid – I never – want to be last
Inmates try to play hard – put on a show,
    I just want to eat – get in – out – and go
All kind of things – being passed here and there,
    Some don't like people close – they're all in
    despair
Things can happen – at the drop of a dime,
    Yelling and hollering – all of the time.
When you're told to leave – and haven't eaten – you throw it away,
    Guards don't care – should' a eaten faster – that's
    what they say.
Can't take it with you – guards watch from their perch,
    Take your food if they find it – when you leave they

do search.

Counts
Every day at three – you must stand on your feet,
    Show your ID – then that counts complete.
Every night at eleven – even if you are asleep,
    There's a light in your eyes – what's up with this creep.
You have to move – and then you just sigh,
    They make sure you're alive – before they go by
At three in the morning – they do it once more,
    As long as they see you – they'll roll by your door.
Seven o'clock in the morning – starts a new day,
    Have to see you move again – before they'll go away.
God forbid they miscount – have to do it once more,
    Instead of two hours – it'll take four.

Revolving Door
There are some inmates here – they keep coming back,
    On the outside – their family – there's something they lack.
All the guards know them – lots of inmates too,
    They have a lot privileges – we see what they do.
When they leave – come back – and hit the ground,
    A lot of inmates get high – drugs all around.
Guards know who they are – see things taking place,
    We all see it happening – it's rights in our face.
Those who keep coming back – are always pat,
    Corruption in corrections – imagine that.

Clichés
Sarah Bousquet

Every sentence has a story
Every person has a past
Every system has corruption
And nothing's built to last
Every liar has a secret
And lies are based on truth
All the clouds have silver linings
but they can't be good for you

There's no time like the present
so live it while you can
Because time gets stolen quickly
When you waste time behind bars

There's no one waiting on you
when you are locked up in a cage
So hold onto your last hopes
and stop counting down the days

There's no place like home
Or so that's what you've been told
But life doesn't work like clichés
so just try to stay alive.

Fertile Concrete
Gary Leaks

Lead and fire, erupted out of the stainless . . . steel weapon of humane destruction
Lead and fire has left a heart broken; a napkin soaked in; tears of grief
Which pours out of the crease of 2 eye sockets
Then rolls down the cheeks of a grieving soul
onto the surface of a sleeping man child
Who open his eyes, then show his grandma his dimples and gummy smile
Then he fills his lungs up with air, ball up his little hands, kick his legs
then allow the church to become acquainted with his presence

In a setting which is sad, the young lad, who never had
the luxury of knowing his dad - Grew up to be a college grad
Through correspondence - Through the walls of correctional institutions
Convicted of murder and drug distribution
Un-consciously volunteered in the destruction of his neighborhood
Because he only knew of no better options . . .
Grew up in a culture of crime
Where money is worshiped and tough guys drop dimes
The world tried to rob him out of his prime
But he primed his mind with knowledge
Now he obtain raw power
I believe that the concrete produced a rose
but all you probably see is a flower.

Lost Souls
Kwame Bias

Lost souls are a man, woman, boy or girl,
that lost his or her way down that trail.
Tryna make a way without seeing a cell,
or a person praying for hope and trying
to get off weed, cocaine, PCP, or dope.
Lost souls cry for help in many ways
just some of them have pride that get in their way
and needing God in their life to get saved.
Lost souls matter every day
some of them need someone to care about them
for a better change.
So people lost souls matter
so think about if it was you climbing down that ladder.

Bad Actors: Sad, Very Sad
Robert Johnson

The sound of metal on metal, grating to you, uh, civilians, makes me feel comfortable, a solid reminder that everything is firmly in its place, secure. A sharp dose of disinfectant smells like home to me. I prefer a small place for one, but a two-man unit, well, that can be cozy too, though the one toilet rule is a constraint. Trust me on that (and don't forget the disinfectant). But when it comes to Correction or, with young guys like me, Reformation, a rundown prison like this one is sweet. Rusted bars, peeling paint, a little funk in the air. Folk on the edge of madness. Man, this gets me in the frame of mind to be bad. Bad conditions, bad company. Good training for the bad life.

Bad to the bone, that's me. At least, that's what I'm meant to be. See this badge? Well, emblem, I guess. Patch. Right here on my shirt. Junior Criminal, Class II, Thug in Training. Means I'm closing in on my First Class Felon Badge. When you make First Class Felon, you're set loose on the world. Not to wreak havoc, exactly, least not directly. See, I'm not a *real* thug. For sure, there are real thugs in the world, but not enough to put a serious scare in people. And many of the real thugs confuse matters by dressing up in business suits and smiling real nice, under-selling good shit and over-selling bad shit, making money flow like honey without much in the way of real work. You know the type. Me, I'm a media creation, a hard-working star in shows like *Criminally Minded* or *CSI Does the Heartland*. If you don't mind my saying so, TV shows are a stretch, but I try to oblige. Gives me a goal, something to work for.

So like I said, when I earn my badge, I'll be a certified replica of a full-on street thug as seen on TV and even on the Silver Screen, and just like magic I'll be released to the streets for a spell. I don't have to do anything, really, just look pretty – pretty mean and scary, that is. That's quite enough. If I can look bad enough, I'll be a walking crime wave.

"Isn't that right," I ask Mr. Murphy, here to my right, one of our counselors, or coaches, as they like to be called. He's pretty cool, considering. No convict, but he knows what's what. At least somewhat. Anyway, he's a big fan of the classic crime text, *The Rich Get Richer and the Poor Get Prison*. Says it's like a prisoner's Bible. Wants us to read a little every day. Good luck with that, right? Murphy's supposed to help us get ready for "reentry," like we're strange-ass aliens coming back into the free world's orbit, which I suppose is true, come to think about it.

"Right, partner," says Murphy, resting his hand on my shoulder. With Murphy, partner sounds like pard-ner, with a slight twang. You know, Texas like. Means you're good people, taken seriously. "I think it's mainly the tats that throw a chill into people," I reply. Tattoos are called tats here in the Reformatory, a prison for young people with a certain kind of promise.

Murphy nods.

"Yeah, Reformatory," I continue, "where we juvenile delinquents are re-formed into something pretty frightening. We come in scared kids and in a few years we're genuinely scary thugs. We look like monsters."

"Monsters with a mission," says Murphy. "That's what this is all about." He's talking like a coach now. He wants us psyched.

"Yeah, damn straight – we scare the straight people, they get bent out of shape, we get another dose of Reformation, and things stay pretty much the same."

"Well, you *do* move up your C Levels," says Murphy, ever the optimist. "Advanced training, stuff like that, when you get back."

C stands for Criminal; there are several criminal levels, First Class Felon being the top rank, means you're ready for the streets. A person who has the rank of First Class Felon, sometimes called Felon First Class, which I like because it has a military ring to it, is one badass foot soldier in the war on crime. You can tell by just looking at him - a full package of tats, colored and plain, like he's a walking billboard of badness. And of course he's got a growing rap sheet he can recite like a résumé, if he knew what a résumé was and how to say it right.

"Don't forget the obligatory guns and pecs" adds Murphy.

"Yeah, big biceps and a full chest. Hard core."

"Chalk it up to cage fitness," says Murphy. "We provide the cages, cons provide the fitness, working out every free minute."

"Free minute?" Gotta call him here.

"Well, free in a manner of speaking. Your choice, right?
"For sure. Fitness matters. Muscles make the man. People on the outs figure you're a hard-ass lowlife if you've got tats and a ripped body. Folks just assume the rap sheet."

"Don't forget the scars," says Murphy. "A matter of some pride—

"Oh, yeah. Scars are big. You get to pick the ones you want. Face scars, they really work; you've got to earn them, though. Understand, a Felon First Class gets scars with the rank. Cheek scars, big and easy to see; sometimes neck scars."

"Tell the whole story," prods Murphy, like we have an audience. He just likes to hear about this stuff, makes him feel like he's an insider, a bad dude. He even uses that term - dude - which sounds lame from an older guy, you know, but I smile. Like I said, he's good people.

"OK," I tell him. "Now none of this is real." He knows this but I figure it can't hurt to remind him. "It's not like we're crazy or nothin'. But you put it together - tats, muscles, and face scars (courtesy of tattoo artists) - man, we scare each other sometimes. So you can imagine how the lames see us."

"Lames," says Murphy to no one in particular, an odd habit of his, "means civilians, citizens."

Like I don't know this.

"Yeah, right, civilians. So the lames catch sight of us and it's 'Where do we go to sign up for the Three Strikes laws.' Or, 'Let the business man do an end run around ethics and maybe fleece a small army of elderly disabled women, but get these scary lowlife bastards out of my sight!'"

"It's kind of like a public service," adds Murphy, "just not the whole public, only the public that can make a buck off prisons."

"Right, Brother Murphy. Amen. There's money to be made in prisons."

"So you can see why prisons went private," says Murphy.

"Duh. I mean, come on, who was hittin' it in the first place. The guards? No way. They're hittin' what they can but not this. Private prisons don't pay so good if you work there, and really, you can't count on a pension. The local politicians expect a tax bonanza but boy, the hidden costs of private pens are something else again."

"So the real winners are the rich cats," says Murphy, "fat cats."

"Investors. Cats with money, big money," I add, though fat cats these days are pretty trim. Physically fit, you know, and tanned. Good hair. Usually. But the real deal, and I'm being a hundred now, the real deal is the rich folk get to use *us* as cover, you know what I mean?

"Now sure," I continue, "there are real street criminals out there, and they're plenty scary, but you've got to keep the supply up with the demand, and the plain fact is, people need to be scared of street crime whenever they walk down the street. That takes a lot of criminals on a lot of streets, man, a lot of criminals loose in the world."

"Street crime," says Murphy, like he's making a paid announcement: "politicians provide the street, we provide the crime."

"Sweet," I say. Man is on a roll.

"If the civilians aren't afraid of the streets, they'll look to the suites." Murphy is something of a poet in his spare time. "And that means carefully cultivated and deployed troops, suitable for media attention, roaming the streets, ready for prime-time coverage, looking the part, like bona fide thugs."

"Bona fide," I repeat. You gotta love my coach. You can tell he's had academic training. He talks funny but he means well.

"A-ten-hut," says a square-jawed prison guard, a loser sent from central casting, dressed in military fatigues, chosen for effect. He'd caught us off guard, so to speak, moving real quiet in is black crepe-soled shoes.

I raise my hand to salute him. He's no more real than me – he's no more a baton-wielding goon than I am a bloodthirsty thug – but he has a job to do and so do I. One day I might have to kick his ass, but that's another day and anyway, with prison stats, an 'assault' can be mostly talk; it's all in the reporting. "Assaults climb to record high in prison." Could be verbal assaults, could be eyeballing. Could be real, blood and all, but anyway, the headline's enough.

Behind him I see two guys, faces screwed up in anger, nostrils flared, upper lips raised, hands formed into claws, pawing at each other like cowardly cats in a Disney cartoon. Or the scared dude in Wizard of Oz. Course, only the old cons remember that one.

"Newbies," I say, trying to hide my contempt. "Could have a little pride, don't you think?"

"They'll get the hang of it," Murphy says, not without a hint of resignation. "Probably white collar types, looking for a little respect." He knows how this place works.

Me, I've got the prison routine down pat. Mostly now I want out. I want to prove I can be a bad actor on the big stage, out in the world; a man of menace, even if I am a bit scared myself. No joke now, guys in prison, bad actors, some of us get stage fright when it comes time to go out in the world. I mean, even with the lessons I get just by being here, I sometimes doubt I can really spook anyone.

And now this immigrant thing. Bad hombres. Real bad, we're told. Heavy competition, man. Pretty soon brown-ass gonna trump badass. Sad. Very sad.

But I'm gonna roll with it. Bottom line: if you look bad, you are bad. Media rules, man. No questions asked. No one stands around long enough to ask. Bad hombres. Bad actors. The more bad, the better. So it's all good. That's what I tell myself.

And on a good day, I look in the mirror and scare myself. That's me, I think, one bad actor, soon to be seen on a street near you.

* My thanks to fellow writers Emily Dalgo, Casey Chiappetta, Susan Nagelsen, and Charles Huckelbury for their comments and suggestions on this story.

Friend or Foe
Khalid Karim

You heard me last night, didn't you?
Just as you listen to me virtually
every night
and day,
though you've never judged me,
others did.
You listen to my rants, my screams,
my stories, my regrets, my dreams,
and more...while others hid.
Your presence was felt day in and day out,
and at times you were so cold
and just as often, hot.
I studied your stern disposition
and while I admired your silent lessons,
I hate your own admission
at least where I'm concerned.
You reminded me of what I left behind
and that made me think often
but not always
and some days
I showed my behind
and rewind
I'd act a fool again
striking you,
slighting you,
but it only hurt me.
Angry, depressed, lonely, scared, berserk: Me
But I can't apologize yet
Too much pride
and yet, dear Prison Cell,
all of me,   you hide
you hinder,   you protect
you made me hate
you made me regret

but you made me reflect.
So no, I won't apologize for meeting you
For vandalizing, decorating, or beating you.
But, I will thank you
for helping me, find me,
the real me
who
would like to leave <u>you</u> behind
Real soon.

The Lockdown
Jevon Jackson

"Your correspondence to the Assistant Administrator and the Deputy Secretary of Corrections was received in my office for review and response. You raise issues of the lockdown and claim it is a ruse to cover for staff shortages."

      Last year, the kind and cordial librarian got
        stabbed with a pair of dissembled blunt nose   scissors-
one, two, threefourfive cuts to the flesh,
      the prisoner who attacked her, weeks prior,
      befell to the hallucinations in his head,
      psychosis, the cold ancient odor that wardens
      have no nose for.

"As you state, you have been incarcerated for many years. You are aware that the Warden has the authority, at any time, to suspend institution operations in order to conduct a search of all or part of an institution."

      I have seen such tiny sinful things
      weevil its way
      into the collective brains of convicts,
      where the barren, stark landscape
      approves us to act like
      jackals and wolverines,
      Warden, the things you are searching for-
          weapons, dope, cellphones
      are less destructive
      than the crown of your Indifference.

"You are also aware that is an emergency occurs that prevents the normal functioning of the institution, the Warden may suspend Administrative Rules or any part of them until the emergency is ended and order is restored to the institution."

      guys have been waiting all week,
      to call their six-year old daughters,

> to call their worried wives,
> to talk to someone who is not against them,
> to reconnect to heartbeats
> and rhythms that swoon the soul,
> but now
> Deprivation grows a tiger head,
> eager to devour us
> once we turn our backs,
> the hope room fades to black
> and we become rocks of jagged sullenness.

"It is at my discretion to make the determination when to bring the institution out of lockdown. While it may have been a single incident that precipitated the lockdown, the reason for the duration was a security matter which I will not discuss further."

> When the librarian was attacked,
> a day after, it was operations as normal;
> when the choir boy hanged himself
> with shredded bedsheets and doomed despair,
> a day after, it was operations as normal;
> when the carpenter killed his cellmate
> by egregious strangulation,
> a day after, it was operations as normal;
>
> but now that your staff are quitting
> en masse,
> emergencies have ascended like
> beacons from a lighthouse,
> and yet, you keep this whole entire place
> drowned and locked in darkness.

A Collection of Sonnets from Death Row
Anthony G. Amsterdam

And the Dumpster Was an Afterthought

Bitch did me good.
She went and spent on crack
the bills to buy the baby's food
again, and said she's never comin' back.

Baby wailed and wouldn't stop.
Hunger's siren screaming in my ear.
Diaper stinking full of slop,
I'd had it up to here.

Okay, I shook the kid a bit.
I didn't mean to do it harm.
I didn't mean its head to hit.
Just meant to turn off that alarm.

But then I panic. Ditch the body. Run.
"Premeditation" says the jury. Murder one.

A Short Life

Been on the street since I was eight.
Mom's a crack whore.
Dad don't calculate.
I needed something more.

Mugged a bitch when I was ten.
Went into juvie small.
Rape gang used me then
till I got six foot tall.

Came out and figured I was due
a debt from hell.
Bought me a .22
and robbed a fucking S & L.

Clerk give me lip. I shot her in the head.
Fart-fast jury trial. Big deal. I'm dead.

Explain Me Felony-Murder

On the Coast, out of cash.
I was heading East to stay.
Out of jail, no place to crash.
Thought I'd hitch it all the way.
No more handbag snatch arrests.
No more flipping out berserk.
Used to bricklay with the best.
East was where I'd find some work.
But the first ride that I caught
was a bad-ass with a plan
and a shotgun and the thought
that he'd need a second man.
No, I couldn't pass that by.
Only maybe God knows why.

    Maybe one a.m. or two,
    we would leave the Interstate,
    take the worst-paved road in view,
    find the worst-lit place to wait.
    I would wave a flash and yelp
    how I'd had some awful wreck.
    When the suckers stopped to help,
    he'd put the shotgun to their neck.

    Never had to shoot no one.
    Just relieve them of their cash.
    Till some guy grabbed for the gun
    and it blew his brains to trash.
    So now they strap me down to die.
    Only maybe God knows why.

Another No-News Visit Day

Five years and ten months gone. All grey.
December makes it six.
Cot head so cold your forearm sticks
and tears another piece of flesh away.

Four thousand pushups plus. July
will make it five, when heat pours in
and bakes you in your skin
like ham hung up to dry.

And now I gotta shit away
another visit day
hearin' what my lawyer has to say.
He got or didn't get another stay.

Can't curse no more, or cry or pray.
Linda and the kids so far away.

The Mitigation Interview

You asking how it was when I was six.
My ma was sick then, lost her looks, her teeth, her hope.
Hooked all day, all night, but ugly woman turning tricks
don't make enough to feed four kids and buy her dope.

You asking how it was when I was eight.
Third foster home. Court took me from the first.
They'd beat me. Second? Chained me to the gate
all night for running off. The third one was the worst;

don't want to talk about it. Yeah, I dig the pitch
you lawyers peddle to the jury: "Sure, he shot
a cop, but look, his young years were a miserable bitch,
so show some mercy. Sentence him to life." That's not

my thing. This cop was messing me. All tough
and in my face. Time comes I've fucking had enough.

Finally, on the Gurney

Past time to go. For fourteen years
my lawyers lugged me through appeals.
They fed me on the hope that sears.
They hid me from the guilt that heals.

I pray the law gods grant them grace.
They've done their job and done it well.
But legal points can't make the case
I'd need to fool the courts of hell.

I killed them. Wife and baby son.
She'd left me, took the boy and run.
I hear them screaming, screams so old
my heart is locked in cancerous cold
of deaths that cannot be undone
and truths that cannot be untold.

About the Editors and Contributors

DANIELLA SKLARZ (Editor-in-Chief) is a senior in American University's Honors Program pursuing a BA in Film & Media Arts with a minor in Justice Studies. She is passionate about creating art that motivates audiences to implement positive changes, both on a personal and public level. Daniella directed *Breaking Ground Monologues*, a compilation of student written pieces about individual's relationships with their bodies. She is an active member in both Delta Gamma Sorority and Delta Kappa Alpha Fraternity. She was named a 2016 Victor Hassine Memorial Scholar. As Editor in Chief of Tacenda Literary Magazine, Daniella is responsible for selecting submissions that best illustrate the impact of the criminal justice system.

ROBERT JOHNSON (Consulting Editor) is a Professor of Justice, Law and Criminology at American University, Editor and Publisher of BleakHouse Publishing, and a widely published and award winning author of books and articles on crime and punishment, including works of social science, law, and fiction. He has testified or testified expert affidavits on capital and other criminal cases in many venues, including US state and federal courts, the U.S. Congress, and the European Commission of Human Rights. He is best known for his book, Death Work: A Study of the Modern Execution Process, which won the Outstanding Book Award of the Academy of Criminal Justice Sciences. Johnson is a Distinguished Alumnus of the Nelson A. Rockefeller College of Public Affairs and Policy, University at Albany, State University of New York.

The following writers are alphabetized by first name

ALAZAJUAN GRAY is a member of Free Minds Book Club & Writing Workshop. He is from Washington, DC. He is currently incarcerated. This is his first publication.

ANNA HASSANYEH studied Law at the University of Westminster and worked for the Crown Prosecution Service in London, England. She has also worked as a teacher. Anna has published short stories in *Writers' Forum*, *Litro Online*, and

Tacenda. She now runs an I.T security company with her husband and spends most of her free time reading and writing.

ANTHONY G. AMSTERDAM been a criminal defense lawyer and a law professor for more than half a century, most recently at NYU. He's worked primarily on capital cases and on constitutional challenges to oppressive features of the criminal justice system (JLWOP, police misconduct, racially discriminatory practices, punishment of status crimes, and so forth). Most of his writing is technical legal stuff (for example, the Trial Manual 6 for the Defense of Criminal Cases (6th ed. 2016), co-authored with Randy Hertz), but he's also written about the interface of law and cognitive science, with a focus on the role of narrative in advocacy (for example, Minding the Law (2000), co-authored with Jerome Bruner).

DORTELL WILLIAMS' passion is for youth diversion. He was privelaged enough to serve as editor-in-chief for an anthology of youth admonishment essays called, Dark Tales From The Dungeons: Horrors From the 'Hood for Youth to Beware. He enjoys writing thought-provoking essays for the public about incarceration. Readers are welcome to email dortellwilliams@gmail.com about his work.

EMILY DALGO is a senior in the University Honors Program pursuing a degree in international studies and a minor in philosophy. Dalgo is the Chief Development Officer of BleakHouse Publishing, the Executive Editor of The World Mind Policy magazine, and was named a 2016 Victor Hassine Memorial Scholar. She is the author of Silent, We Sit, an original book of poetry published by BleakHouse in 2016.

GARY LEAKS is a member of Free Minds Book Club & Writing Workshop. He is from Washington, DC. He is currently incarcerated in federal prison. This is his first publication. If you wish to learn more about Gary, please contact Free Minds (mail@freemindsbookclub.org) for his contact information.

HALIM A. FLOWERS has published ten books, of which three are poetry collections titled A Reason To Breathe: Volumes I & II and Buried Alive: Dead Men Do Talk. A native of the District of Columbia, he was first inspired to write at the age of seven in the second grade at Kingsman Elementary School. The poem "I Will Cry For The Little Boy" was inspired by Antwone Fisher's poem titled "Who Will Cry For The Little Boy?" Halim now focuses on writing socially conscious short fiction and poetry. You can follow him on Facebook (Halim A. Flowers), Instagram (@halimflowers), Twitter (@therealhalim) or read his blog entries on Tumblr (Ideallionaires.tumblr.com) and at ConvictSoapbox.com.

HANNAH EHLERS graduated from American University in 2016 with a BA in Jewish Studies. During her sophomore year, she was Editor in Chief of Tacenda. Currently, Ehlers is a corp member of Avodah, the Jewish Service Corps. Through Avodah, she is a Program Coordinator at DC SCORES, a non-profit organization that provides after school programming in soccer, poetry, and service – learning to under-resourced youth in DC. Ehlers has done work related to many social justice issues, including criminal justice reform, education justice and Israeli- Palestinian peace.

JEAN MARC AKERELE is a member of Free Minds Book Club & Writing Workshop. He is from Washington, DC. He is currently incarcerated in federal prison. This is his first publication.

JEVON JACKSON has published two books of poetry entitled *Why the Prisoner Only Writes Love Poems* and *Handwritten Poems* online with PrisonsFoundation.org. His poems also appear in the publications *J Journal* and *The Oyez Review*. Jevon is an ambassador and correspondent for *The Community News*, a publication out of Milwaukee, Wisconsin. He is co-author of the in-progress book, *Between Writers and Lifers*. Jevon currently resides in the New Lisbon Correctional Institution in Wisconsin.

JOSEF KREBS has a chapbook published by Etched Press and his poetry also appears in *Agenda, the Bicycle Review, Calliope, Mouse Tales Press, The Corner Club Press, The FictionWeek Literary Review, Burningword Literary Journal, the Aurorean, Inscape, Crack the Spine, The Cape Rock,Carcinogenic Poetry, The Bangalore Review, 521magazine,* and *The Cats Meow*. A short story has been published in blazeVOX. He's written three novels and five screenplays. His film was successfully screened at Santa Cruz and Short Film Corner of Cannes film festivals.

KARI LORENTSON graduated from American University in 2015 with a BA in Political Science. She is currently pursuing her J.D. at the University of Notre Dame.

KHALID KARIM is a Washington, DC native who's made brief stays in VA, MD, and even St Croix (US Virgin Island). He comes from a large family and holds them and friendships in high regard. And though his life has had its fair share of hardships, he's learned to grow from these lessons. He's been incarcerated for the past 24 years but he's not been inactive. Most of his time has been spent mentoring, reading, writing, and working to fulfill his own dreams. As a poet, he has been featured in the Beat Within and Tacenda publications. He is currently self-publishing his own book of poetry titled, "I was Just Thinking." He will continue to write, mentor, and evolve, in the hopes of doing more for others, as others have done for him because he understands that he owes.

KWAME BIAS is a member of Free Minds Book Club & Writing Workshop. He is from Washington, DC. He is currently incarcerated in federal prison. This is his first publication.

LAWRENCE GREEN is a member of Free Minds Book Club & Writing Workshop. He is currently incarcerated. This is his first publication.

LUCAS CHAPMAN studied issues in criminal justice with Dr. Robert Johnson. He graduated from American University in May of 2016 with a Bachelor's Degree in History, and is currently working as a combat medic in Syria.

LYDELL CLANTON is a member of Free Minds Book Club & Writing Workshop. He is from Washington, DC. He is currently incarcerated in federal prison. This is his first publication.

MAUREEN GERAGHTY has been teaching in alternative school settings for 26 years. She and her two school-aged children live in Portland, Oregon. She self-published a book of poetry entitled,

Look Up- Poems of a Life and has poetry published in *ReThinking Schools,* mamazine.com, mothering.com and *Teaching with Heart.* Her essay, "Our Better Angels," will appear in the anthology *Watch My Rising.* She and Jevon published an article, "Writing Outside the Bars" with the National Writing Project's journal, *The Quarterly,* which is a portion of a book they are currently working on, entitled *Between Writers and Lifers.*

NANCY TOLLEY is an active member of the Maryland Correctional Institute for Women Book and Writers Club. Along with attending day courses offered through Anne Arundel Community College, she attends Goucher college in the evenings. She is passionate about both reading and writing. Her goal is to become a freelance writer.

NAOMI ZEIGLER is an undergraduate student at American University majoring in literature with minors in political science and women's studies. A staunch opponent of capital punishment, she has interned with the Death Penalty Information Center in Washington DC and hopes to continue in abolition advocacy throughout her life. Naomi loves intersectional feminism, politics, art museums, film, dogs and Earl Grey tea.

NASTASYA POPOV is a senior studying Film and Creative Nonfiction at Northwestern University. Her short story, "Terminal Island" and her essay "The Mother Art" have both received Northwestern English Department Awards. (A stranger she met on a bus to the airport in Chicago informed her that "the Russians, genetically, have a high tolerance for suffering," and she strives to use that assertion in her writing.) She writes about her personal experience with having a parent in prison, about criminal justice on a larger scale, and about life's fascinating incongruities.

NICK LEININGER is a Public Relations and Marketing student at American University. After graduating in May he hopes to stay involved in the arts and become a full-fledged Washingtonian. In his spare time he likes to explore the various museums and art galleries of DC, partake in physical activity, and continue his quest for the perfect cold brew coffee. Nick is currently interning at The John F. Kennedy Center for the Performing Arts. Poetry is Nick's preferred medium of self-expression. He believes that poetry is where he can accurately express his true self in the most elegant way possible.

RICK LYON'S book BELL 8 was published by BOA Editions. His work has appeared in COLORADO REVIEW, THE NATION and THE NEW REPUBLIC. He's a boat captain from Connecticut, originally, and now a truck driver. He lives with his wife Lisa LeVally on a horse farm in Des Plaines, Illinois.

RYAN NEWMAN is a member of Free Minds Book Club & Writing Workshop. He is from Washington, DC. He is currently incarcerated in federal prison. This is his first publication.

SARAH BOUSQUET is a graduate of American University with a Bachelor's degree in Justice and Law. Her publications include BleakHouse Review (2013, 2014) as well as the MDPI Law Journal Special Issue: The Death Penalty in the 21st Century (Death House Desiderata: A Hunger for Justice). She won awards for Best Poem with BleakHouse Publishing in 2013 and 2014. She currently lives in Australia.

SINCERE ECHOES or Shawndell, who writes under the penname "Sincere Echoes," is a member of Free Minds Book Club & Writing Workshop. He is currently incarcerated in federal prison. This is his first publication.

TIMOTHY TINGLE-BROWN is a member of Free Minds Book Club & Writing Workshop. He is currently incarcerated in federal prison. This is his first publication.